WHAT ARE THE BOOKS OF EZRA & NEHEMIAH?

Kids' Guides to God's Word Series

What Is the Book of Genesis?
What Is the Book of Exodus?
What Is the Book of Leviticus?
What Is the Book of Numbers?
What Is the Book of Deuteronomy?
What Is the Book of Joshua?
What Is the Book of Judges?
What Is the Book of Ruth?
What Is the Book of 1 Samuel?
What Is the Book of 2 Samuel?
What Is the Book of 1 Kings?
What Is the Book of 2 Kings?
What Are the Books of 1–2 Chronicles?
What Are the Books of Ezra & Nehemiah?
What Is the Book of Esther?
What Is the Book of Job?
What Is the Book of Psalms?
What Is the Book of Proverbs?
What Is the Book of Ecclesiastes?
*What Are the Books of Song of Songs &
Lamentations?*
What Is the Book of Isaiah?
What Is the Book of Jeremiah?
What Is the Book of Ezekiel?
What Is the Book of Daniel?
What Are the Books of Hosea–Micah?
What Are the Books of Nahum–Malachi?

What Is the Gospel of Matthew?
What Is the Gospel of Mark?
What Is the Gospel of Luke?
What Is the Gospel of John?
What Is the Book of Acts?
What Is the Book of Romans?
What Is the Book of 1 Corinthians?
What Is the Book of 2 Corinthians?
What Is the Book of Galatians?
What Is the Book of Ephesians?
What Is the Book of Philippians?
*What Are the Books of Colossians
& Philemon?*
What Are the Books of 1–2 Thessalonians?
What Are the Books of 1–2 Timothy & Titus?
What Is the Book of Hebrews?
What Is the Book of James?
What Are the Books of 1–2 Peter & Jude?
What Are the Books of 1-3 John?
What Is the Book of Revelation?

What Are the Books of

EZRA & NEHEMIAH?

Michael Whitworth

ISBN 978-1-971767-23-9

Published by Start2Finish
Bend, Oregon 97702
start2finish.org

Printed in the United States of America
30 29 28 27 26   1 2 3 4 5

CONTENTS

INTRODUCTION

Have you ever tried to rebuild something that was broken? Maybe it was a friendship that fell apart after a fight. Maybe it was your confidence after a failure that embarrassed you in front of everyone. Maybe your family went through something hard—a move, a divorce, a loss—and afterward you had to figure out how to put the pieces of your life back together in a way that made sense.

Here's what nobody tells you about rebuilding: it's harder than building the first time. When you build something new, you start with a blank page and fresh excitement. When you rebuild, you start with rubble. You start with the memory of what used to be there. You start with the knowledge that it broke once and could break again. Rebuilding takes a different kind of courage, the kind that picks up a hammer when every part of you wants to walk away.

That's what the books of Ezra and Nehemiah are about. They tell the story of a people trying to rebuild everything: their city, their temple, their walls, their identity, and their relationship with God. And the rebuilding is harder than anyone expected. The rubble is real. The enemies are relentless. The people's own hearts keep drifting back to the habits that destroyed them in the first place. It's a story of extraordinary faith, stunning failure, and stubborn grace.

And it's one of the most important stories in the Bible, even though most people have never read it.

WHERE WE'VE BEEN

To understand Ezra and Nehemiah, you need to know what came before. And what came before was a catastrophe.

For centuries, the nation of Israel had been God's chosen people. He had rescued them from slavery in Egypt, given them his law at Mount Sinai, led them into the Promised Land, and established a kingdom under David and Solomon. Solomon built a magnificent temple in Jerusalem, and God's presence filled it. For a brief, shining moment, everything God had promised Abraham seemed to be coming true.

Then it all fell apart. The kingdom split in two. The northern kingdom abandoned God entirely and was conquered by Assyria. The southern kingdom, Judah, held on longer but eventually followed the same path: idolatry, injustice, and stubborn refusal to listen to the prophets God sent to warn them. Finally, in 586 BC, the Babylonian Empire destroyed Jerusalem, burned the temple to the ground, and dragged the people into exile.

For roughly seventy years, God's people lived in a foreign land. The temple was gone. The city was rubble. The promises of Abraham, David, and the prophets seemed dead.

But they weren't. God had told the prophet Jeremiah that the exile would last seventy years, and then he would bring his people home. And that's exactly what happened. The Babylonian Empire fell to Persia, and a Persian king named Cyrus issued a decree that the Jews could return to Jerusalem and rebuild.

Ezra and Nehemiah tell the story of that return and that rebuilding. It unfolds in three major waves across roughly a hundred years, and each wave has its own leader, its own challenges, and its own lessons.

WHAT YOU'RE ABOUT TO READ

The first wave came under Zerubbabel, around 538 BC. A group of roughly 42,000 exiles made the long journey back to Jerusalem, rebuilt the altar, and eventually completed a new temple, though not without years of opposition and delay. You'll read about a pagan king whose heart God stirred, a foundation-laying ceremony where the old people wept and the young people cheered at the same time, enemies who tried to shut the project down, and prophets who stirred the people back to work after sixteen years of giving up.

The second wave came under Ezra, around 458 BC. Ezra was a priest and scholar who devoted his life to studying, obeying, and teaching God's law. He arrived in Jerusalem carrying a fortune in gold and silver, protected not by soldiers but by prayer and fasting. What he found when he got there shattered him: the people had intermarried with the surrounding nations, repeating the very pattern that had led to the exile in the first place. His grief-stricken response and the painful reckoning that followed are some of the most intense chapters in the Old Testament.

The third wave came under Nehemiah, around 445 BC. Nehemiah was the cupbearer to the Persian king, a man with access to the most powerful ruler on earth. When he heard that Jerusalem's walls were still in ruins, he wept, prayed for four months, and then boldly asked the king for permission to go rebuild them. What followed was a fifty-two-day construction project carried out under constant threat: mockery, conspiracy, assassination attempts, and sabotage from every direction. The builders worked with swords at their belts and trowels in their hands.

But the story doesn't end with the wall going up. It ends with Nehemiah leaving Jerusalem and returning to find that nearly every promise the people made has been broken. The temple has been compromised. The sabbath is being ignored. The intermarriages are back. The book closes not with a triumph but with a prayer: "Remember me, O my God, for good."

WHY THESE BOOKS MATTER

You might be wondering why two books about ancient construction projects and census lists matter to your life. Here's why: Ezra and Nehemiah answer a question you've probably already started asking, even if you don't have words for it yet.

The question is this: Why can't we just be good?

Every person who has ever tried to keep a New Year's resolution, maintain a habit, or stay committed to something they know is right understands this problem. You start strong. You mean it. You really do. But then the enthusiasm fades, the distractions pile up, and before you know it, you're right back where you started.

That's the story of God's people in Ezra and Nehemiah. They return from exile full of gratitude and good intentions. They rebuild the temple. They renew the covenant. They make specific, public promises to follow God's law. And then, within a generation, they break every single one.

These books are painfully honest about human failure. But they're also radiant with something else: the faithfulness of God. In every chapter, behind every setback and through every act of rebuilding, God is at work. He stirs the hearts of pagan kings. He protects caravans on dangerous roads. He watches over builders surrounded by enemies. He sends prophets to restart what fear has stalled. He uses imperfect leaders to accomplish his purposes.

And he keeps pointing the story forward. Because if exile couldn't fix the human heart, and the Law couldn't fix it, and the strongest leaders couldn't fix it, then something else, someone else, was needed. Ezra and Nehemiah set the stage for the New Testament by making the need for Jesus unmistakably clear.

BEFORE YOU BEGIN

A few things to keep in mind as you read.

These books are full of lists: names of families, inventories of temple articles, sections of wall assigned to different groups. It's tempting to skip those parts, but they matter. Every name represents a real person who said yes when saying yes was costly. Every list is a reminder that God sees individuals, not just crowds.

The opposition is real and relentless. Enemies mock, threaten, scheme, bribe, and infiltrate. If you've ever tried to do something good and been surprised by how hard people pushed back, you'll recognize what's happening in these pages.

The morality is sometimes uncomfortable. The intermarriage crisis and its resolution involve real families being torn apart. The text doesn't pretend this was painless. We'll walk through it honestly.

And the ending is unresolved. These books don't close with trumpets and celebration. They close with a broken leader asking God to remember him. That's not a failure of storytelling. It's the honest truth about where the Old Testament leaves us: waiting for someone who can do what walls and laws and willpower cannot.

LET'S BEGIN

So here we are, about to follow a group of exiles on the long road back to a city that exists only in their grandparents' memories. We'll watch them lay foundations and dodge enemies. We'll see them weep over Scripture and celebrate in the streets. We'll watch them make promises and break them. And through it all, we'll see a God who never stops rebuilding, never stops pursuing, and never stops being faithful, even when his people aren't.

The rubble is waiting. The hammer is in your hand. Let's go to Jerusalem.

Turn the page.

1

THE ROAD HOME

When Mary Lennox first arrives at Misselthwaite Manor in Frances Hodgson Burnett's *The Secret Garden*, she finds a place that feels dead. The sprawling estate on the English moors is cold, dark, and unwelcoming. Doors are locked. Rooms are shut up. The servants don't smile. And somewhere behind a hidden door in a high stone wall, there's a garden that nobody has entered in ten years. It was once the most beautiful place on the property, full of climbing roses and green, living things. But after tragedy struck, the master of the house locked the door, buried the key, and tried to forget it ever existed.

The garden didn't disappear. It was still there behind the wall, overgrown and neglected, waiting. And when Mary finally finds the key and pushes open that door, she discovers something astonishing: life is still in the soil. Beneath the weeds and dead wood, green shoots are pushing up. The garden isn't dead. It's been sleeping. And all it needs is someone willing to come back, clear away the ruin, and let the light in again.

That's a picture of what's happening in the first two chapters of Ezra. A place that was once the center of the world for God's people, a place of worship and promise and beauty, has been lying in ruins for decades. The temple in Jerusalem was destroyed. The city's walls were torn down. The people who once filled its streets with singing and sacrifice were dragged away to a foreign land. And for roughly seventy years, the rubble just sat there. Silent. Overgrown. Forgotten by everyone, it seemed.

But not by God. God never forgot Jerusalem. And in Ezra 1, he picks up the key, unlocks the door, and invites his people to come home.

SEVENTY YEARS OF SILENCE

To understand why this moment matters so much, you need to know what came before it.

About seventy years earlier, the unthinkable had happened. The Babylonian Empire, led by a ruthless king named Nebuchadnezzar, had invaded the kingdom of Judah, besieged Jerusalem, and burned it to the ground. The temple that Solomon had built, the place where God's presence dwelled among his people, was destroyed. The walls were smashed. The gold and silver articles used in worship were hauled away as war trophies and placed in the temple of a Babylonian god named Marduk.

And the people themselves were carried off into exile. The best and brightest, the leaders and priests, the skilled workers and artisans, were marched hundreds of miles east to Babylon. They were foreigners in a strange land, surrounded by foreign gods and foreign customs, cut off from everything that made them who they were.

The prophets had warned them this would happen. For years, Jeremiah had stood in the streets of Jerusalem and told the people that if they didn't turn back to God, judgment was coming. They didn't listen. And judgment came.

But Jeremiah also said something else. He said the exile wouldn't last forever. God told his people through Jeremiah, "When seventy years are completed for Babylon, I will come to you and fulfill my good promise to bring you back to this place" (Jeremiah 29:10). Even in the middle of announcing punishment, God was already promising restoration.

The question was: would he keep that promise?

GOD MOVES A KING

Ezra 1 answers that question with the most unlikely opening sentence in the Old Testament. "In the first year of Cyrus king of Persia, in order to fulfill the word of the Lord spoken by Jeremiah, the Lord moved the heart of Cyrus king of Persia to make a proclamation throughout his realm and also to put it in writing."

Read that carefully. The Lord *moved the heart* of a pagan king.

Cyrus was the ruler of the Persian Empire, the most powerful man on earth. He had conquered Babylon in 539 BC, toppling the empire that had destroyed Jerusalem. He was not a worshiper of Israel's God. He didn't read the Scriptures. He didn't attend synagogue. He worshiped his own gods and ran his empire by his own rules.

And yet God reached into the heart of this man and stirred him to do something extraordinary: send the Jewish exiles home.

Here's what Cyrus proclaimed: "The Lord, the God of heaven, has given me all the kingdoms of the earth and he has appointed me to build a temple for him at Jerusalem in Judah. Any of his people among you may go up to Jerusalem in Judah and build the temple of the Lord, the God of Israel."

Now, was Cyrus a true believer? Almost certainly not. Archaeologists have found a clay cylinder, called the Cyrus Cylinder, that shows Cyrus made similar proclamations for other peoples and their gods too. It was his political strategy: instead of crushing conquered peoples and forcing them to forget their identity (the way the Babylonians had operated), Cyrus let people go home, rebuild their temples, and worship their own gods. He figured they'd be more loyal that way.

But here's what the author of Ezra wants you to see: Cyrus had his political reasons. God had his own reasons. And God's reasons are the ones that actually matter. Cyrus thought he was being a clever politician. In reality, he was a tool in the hand of the living God, fulfilling a promise made through a prophet decades earlier. The most powerful man on earth was being directed by someone far more powerful, and he didn't even know it.

That's how God works. He doesn't need people to understand his plan in order to use them in his plan.

A SECOND EXODUS

The decree went out across the empire. And then something happened that was just as miraculous as the decree itself: people actually got up and went.

Think about what that decision meant. These families had been in Babylon for decades. Many of them had been born there. They had homes, businesses, routines. Babylon was one of the most impressive cities in the ancient world, with massive walls, lush gardens, and a thriving economy. Jerusalem, by contrast, was a pile of rubble surrounded by hostile neighbors. There was no temple, no functioning government, no infrastructure. Going "home" meant going to a place most of them had never seen, to start from scratch in dangerous conditions.

Not everyone went. In fact, most didn't. The majority of the Jewish population stayed in Babylon where life was comfortable. But the text says that "everyone whose heart God had moved" prepared to go. Just as God had stirred the heart of Cyrus to issue the decree, God stirred the hearts of specific people to respond to it. God was working on both ends: opening the door and then moving people to walk through it.

The ones who stayed behind didn't just wave goodbye. They loaded up the travelers with silver, gold, goods, livestock, and offerings for the temple. If you've read the book of Exodus, this might sound familiar. When the Israelites left Egypt centuries earlier, their neighbors sent them away loaded with valuables too. The author of Ezra wants you to catch that echo. This isn't just a political relocation. This is a second exodus. God is rescuing his people and bringing them home, just like he did before.

THE TREASURE COMES HOME

And then Cyrus did something that must have sent chills down the spine of every Jewish person who heard about it. He brought out the gold and silver articles that Nebuchadnezzar had stolen from the temple and placed in the house of his Babylonian god. Thirty gold dishes. A thousand silver dishes. Gold bowls, silver bowls, and hundreds of other articles, 5,400 pieces in all. Every single one of them was counted out, piece by piece, and handed over to a Jewish leader named Sheshbazzar.

These weren't just valuable objects. They were symbols. When Nebuchadnezzar took them from the temple and put them in Marduk's temple, it was a statement: *our god beat your God.* Now those same articles were being carried out of Babylon and back to Jerusalem. The statement was being reversed. God hadn't lost. He had never lost. He had allowed his people to be disciplined, but he never abandoned his promises. And now the proof was in their hands, gleaming in the sunlight, headed home.

THE PEOPLE WHO SAID YES

Then comes the part of Ezra that most people skip: the list. Ezra 2 is a long chapter of names and numbers. Families and clans, priests and Levites, temple servants and gatekeepers, all listed by name with the number of people in each group. If you tried to read it straight through, your eyes would probably glaze over around verse ten.

But don't skip it. Because this list is one of the most important chapters in the book.

Here's why: these are the names of the people who said yes.

When God opened the door to go home, when the decree went out and the choice was laid before every Jewish family in Babylon, these are the people who packed up their lives, left behind everything familiar, and walked eight hundred miles into an uncertain future because they believed God's promises were worth more than Babylon's comfort.

The list includes leaders like Zerubbabel and Jeshua, who would guide the community and eventually rebuild the temple. It includes ordinary families identified by their ancestors. It includes people identified by the towns they came from. It includes priests who would restart the sacrificial system, Levites who would serve in the temple, singers who would lead worship, and gatekeepers who would guard the doors. It even includes temple servants, people who did the unglamorous behind-the-scenes work that kept everything running.

The total count was 42,360 people, plus over 7,000 servants, plus singers, plus horses, mules, camels, and donkeys. This was not a small caravan. It was a massive, noisy, complicated migration of people who believed that a ruined city and an empty hill were worth more than the most impressive empire on earth, because God had said so.

WHO BELONGS?

There's a detail near the end of the list that's easy to miss but important. Some people showed up who couldn't prove they belonged. They claimed to be Israelites, but they had lost their family records during the exile. And a few men claimed to be priests but couldn't prove their ancestry. The leader told them they couldn't serve as priests until a proper priest could consult God about it using the ancient method of the Urim and Thummim.

Why does this matter? Because identity mattered to this community. They weren't just rebuilding a city. They were rebuilding a people. They needed to know who they were and where they came from, because their identity as God's covenant people was the foundation everything else would be built on. You can't rebuild the house of God if you don't know who the people of God are.

HOME AT LAST

The chapter ends with the people arriving and settling in their towns. Some of the family leaders gave generous freewill offerings to fund the rebuilding of the temple, giving gold, silver, and priestly garments. Then the people spread out across the land, priests and Levites near Jerusalem, everyone else in the towns their families had lived in before the exile.

They were home. The soil was still there. The green shoots were still alive beneath the surface. And the work of restoration was about to begin.

WHAT THIS MEANS FOR US

First, God keeps his promises, even when it takes longer than we'd like. Seventy years is a long time. Most of the people who heard Jeremiah's original prophecy didn't live to see it fulfilled. But God didn't forget. He never does. If God has made a promise, you can count on it, even if the timing doesn't match your expectations.

Second, God can use anyone to accomplish his purposes. Cyrus wasn't a believer. He didn't know he was fulfilling biblical prophecy. He thought he was just running his empire. But God used him anyway. That should change how you look at the world around you. God isn't limited to working through people who know him. He's sovereign over presidents and principals, coaches and classmates, even people who have never opened a Bible.

Third, following God sometimes means leaving comfort behind. The Jews who returned to Jerusalem gave up safe, established lives in Babylon for the uncertainty of a ruined homeland. Following God doesn't always lead to the easiest path. Sometimes it leads to the hardest one. But it always leads to the right one.

Fourth, everyone's contribution matters. The list in Ezra 2 includes famous leaders and nameless servants. It includes priests who would lead worship and gatekeepers who would watch doors. Nobody's role was too small to be recorded. God saw every person who said yes, and he wrote their names down. He sees your faithfulness too, even when it feels invisible.

Fifth, knowing who you are matters. The returning exiles cared deeply about identity, about knowing whose they were and where they belonged. In a world that will try to tell you your identity comes from your popularity, your grades, your appearance, or your social media following, the Bible says your identity comes from belonging to God. That's the foundation everything else gets built on.

TALKING POINTS

1. **God "moved the heart" of Cyrus to issue the decree, and he "moved the hearts" of certain Jews to respond.** What does it mean that God works on both sides of a situation? Can you think of a time when circumstances and your own desires seemed to line up in a way that felt bigger than coincidence?

2. **Most of the Jews in Babylon chose to stay rather than return to Jerusalem.** Why do you think comfort and familiarity are so powerful? What makes it hard to follow God when it means giving up something easy for something uncertain?

3. **The temple articles that Nebuchadnezzar stole were returned under Cyrus.** What do you think it meant to the Jewish people to see those items coming home? What does it tell us about how God handles things that seem permanently lost?

4. **Ezra 2 is a long list of names that most people skip.** Why do you think God included it in the Bible? What does it say about how God views ordinary, faithful people? How does it make you feel to know that God pays attention to who shows up?

5. **Some people in the list couldn't prove their family identity and were temporarily excluded from certain roles.** Why was identity so important to this community? What are the things that truly define who you are?

The road home has begun. The exiles are back in the land. The temple articles are gleaming in the Jerusalem sun for the first time in seventy years. But the hardest part is still ahead. A foundation needs to be laid, walls need to go up, and not everyone in the neighborhood is happy about it.

Turn the page.

2

THE TEMPLE THAT ALMOST WASN'T

When Alice returns to Underland in Tim Burton's *Alice in Wonderland*, she doesn't recognize the place. The world she once knew is ruined. The Red Queen has seized power, and her reign has twisted everything. The trees are dead. The creatures are oppressed. The Hatter has gone mad with grief. The whole land is waiting for someone to come and set things right.

And everyone tells Alice she's the one. There's a scroll that says so. A prophecy. She's supposed to slay the Jabberwocky and restore the White Queen to the throne. But Alice doesn't believe it. She's spent most of the movie insisting she's in a dream, that none of this is real, that she's not the right person for the job. She's overwhelmed by the scale of what's been destroyed and terrified by the enemy she's supposed to face.

But here's the thing about Underland: it was never really up to Alice. The land had been waiting to be restored long before she arrived. The loyal creatures had been holding on. The White Queen had never stopped believing. And when Alice finally stops running and picks up the sword, the victory isn't just about her courage. It's about a restoration that was always coming, because the rightful queen had never actually lost her claim to the throne.

That's a picture of what happens in Ezra 3–6. The Jewish exiles returned to a land in ruins. The temple was gone. The enemies were powerful. And the people who were supposed to rebuild it were overwhelmed, afraid, and eventually gave up for sixteen years. The half-built temple just sat there, unfinished, while the people focused on their own lives.

But the restoration was never really up to them. God had been planning it long before they picked up a single stone. And the fact that the temple was eventually completed, despite every obstacle, tells us something important: God finishes what he starts, even when his people don't.

FIRST THINGS FIRST

The exiles had barely settled into their towns when they gathered together in Jerusalem. It was the seventh month, and they had something urgent to do before anything else: rebuild the altar.

Not the temple. The altar.

That's a detail worth noticing. Before they laid a single stone for the temple walls, before they drew up building plans or organized construction crews, the first thing they built was the altar of burnt offering. Why? Because the altar was where sacrifices happened. It was where the people connected with God, offered their worship, and received forgiveness for their sins. Without the altar, nothing else mattered. The temple was important, but worship came first.

Two leaders stepped forward to oversee the project: Jeshua the high priest and Zerubbabel the governor. Together they built the altar "in accordance with what is written in the Law of Moses." That phrase matters. They weren't making things up as they went. They weren't adapting their worship to fit the culture around them. They went straight back to the instructions God had given Moses centuries earlier and followed them to the letter.

But here's the thing that makes this moment so remarkable. The text says they built the altar "despite their fear of the peoples around them." They were afraid. The neighboring populations, people who had been living in the land while the Jews were in exile, were not happy to see them back. These neighbors were hostile, and the returning exiles knew it. But they built the altar anyway. They worshiped God in the middle of their fear, not after it went away.

Once the altar was in place, the sacrifices resumed. Morning and evening, every single day. Then came the Festival of Tabernacles, one of Israel's great annual celebrations. Burnt offerings, new moon sacrifices, freewill offerings. The rhythm of worship that had been silent for seventy years was beating again.

JOY AND TEARS

About seven months after arriving in Jerusalem, the people were ready for the next step: laying the foundation of the temple itself. They hired stonecutters and carpenters. They brought cedar logs from Lebanon, just as Solomon had done when he built the original temple centuries earlier. And in the second month of the second year, with the Levites supervising and the priests in their robes with trumpets and cymbals, the work began.

When the foundation was finally laid, the people erupted. The priests blew trumpets. The Levites crashed cymbals. The whole assembly sang together, "He is good; his love to Israel endures forever." It was the same psalm that had been sung when Solomon dedicated the first temple. The shout of praise was so loud it could be heard from far away.

But not everyone was shouting for joy.

Some of the older people, the ones who had actually seen Solomon's temple before Nebuchadnezzar destroyed it, stood there and wept. They could see that this new foundation was not going to produce anything close to the original. Solomon's temple had been one of the wonders of the ancient world, covered in gold and filled with magnificent craftsmanship. This was going to be simpler. Smaller. Less.

So the sound that echoed across Jerusalem that day was a strange and beautiful mix: shouts of joy from the younger generation who saw new beginnings, and sobs of grief from the older generation who remembered what had been lost. Nobody could tell the difference between the two because they all blended together into one enormous noise.

That's an honest picture of what restoration often looks like. It's not pure celebration. There's joy because God is doing something new, and there's grief because the old thing is gone and the new thing isn't quite the same. Both responses are real. Both are valid. And God was present in both of them.

THE ENEMIES ARRIVE

The noise got the attention of people the exiles didn't want noticing them. The text calls them "the enemies of Judah and

Benjamin," though they didn't introduce themselves that way. They came to Zerubbabel with a friendly offer: "Let us help you build. We worship your God too. We've been sacrificing to him ever since the king of Assyria brought us here."

This sounds reasonable on the surface. More hands means faster work, right? But Zerubbabel and the other leaders saw through it. These people had been planted in the land by the Assyrians generations earlier, and while they claimed to worship God, their worship was mixed with the worship of other gods. Letting them join the project would have corrupted the very thing the exiles were trying to rebuild. A temple for the Lord had to be built by the people of the Lord.

So Zerubbabel said no. "You have no part with us in building a temple to our God. We alone will build it for the Lord, the God of Israel, as King Cyrus commanded us."

The rejection did not go over well. What had been a friendly offer turned into open hostility. The people around them launched a campaign of intimidation. They discouraged the builders. They frightened them. They hired officials to work against them behind the scenes, lobbying the Persian court to shut the project down. The harassment wasn't a one-time event; it was constant, grinding pressure that went on for years.

And it worked. The people got scared. The enthusiasm drained away. The work slowed. And then it stopped.

SIXTEEN YEARS OF SILENCE

For sixteen years, the half-finished temple sat abandoned. The foundation was there, but the walls were not. The altar still stood, but the building that was supposed to surround it remained an empty construction site.

What happened? Fear played a role, certainly. The opposition from the neighboring peoples was real and relentless. But the prophet Haggai, who would later show up to confront the situation, pointed to something else: the people had gotten comfortable. While the temple sat unfinished, they were busy building nice houses for themselves. They had paneled walls and comfortable lives while God's house was a pile of rubble. Their priorities had shifted. The urgency they felt when they first arrived had faded into something closer to apathy.

It's easy to judge them for this. But be honest: haven't you ever started something important with great enthusiasm and then quietly let it die? A new habit, a commitment to pray every day, a friendship you meant to invest in? The gap between good intentions and follow-through is enormous, and sixteen years can pass faster than you think when you're distracted by your own comfort.

TWO PROPHETS BREAK THE SILENCE

Then God did something. He sent two prophets.

Haggai and Zechariah arrived on the scene and started preaching. Haggai was blunt and direct, pointing out that the people's crops were failing and their money was disappearing because they had abandoned God's house. "Is it a time for you yourselves to be living in your paneled houses, while this house remains a ruin?" he demanded. Zechariah was more visionary, painting pictures of what God would do through this temple and the future it pointed toward.

Between the two of them, something shifted. Zerubbabel and Jeshua were stirred up again. The people were stirred up again. And the work restarted.

This time, things would be different.

INVESTIGATED BUT NOT STOPPED

Almost immediately, trouble showed up again. A Persian official named Tattenai, the governor of the entire region, came to Jerusalem and demanded answers. "Who authorized you to rebuild this temple? What are your names?"

These were dangerous questions. Names meant accountability. If the work wasn't authorized, names meant punishment.

But the text adds a crucial sentence: "The eye of their God was watching over the elders of the Jews, and they were not stopped."

This time, instead of shutting down in fear, the Jewish leaders stood their ground. They gave Tattenai a calm, confident answer. They explained their history: how Solomon had built the original temple, how their ancestors' sin had led to its destruction under Nebuchadnezzar, how Cyrus had issued a decree authorizing them to rebuild, and how Sheshbazzar had laid the foundation years earlier. Then they invited Tattenai to go check the royal archives himself.

Tattenai did exactly that. He wrote to King Darius, laid out the situation, and asked him to search the records for Cyrus' original decree.

And while they waited for the reply, the Jews kept building.

THE DECREE CONFIRMED

Darius ordered a search. The officials looked through the archives in Babylon and eventually found the document in Ecbatana, the Persian summer capital, where Cyrus had been staying when he issued it. The original decree was right there in black and white: rebuild the temple in Jerusalem, pay for it from the royal treasury, and return the stolen temple articles.

Darius didn't just confirm the decree. He added to it. He ordered Tattenai and his officials to stay away from the construction site, to fund the project from regional tax revenues, and to provide whatever the priests needed for sacrifices, including bulls, rams, lambs, wheat, salt, wine, and oil. And he added a threat: anyone who interfered with the decree would have a beam ripped from his own house and be impaled on it.

The very investigation that could have shut the project down became the thing that guaranteed its completion. What the enemies meant to use as a weapon, God turned into a shield.

FINISHED

The temple was completed on the third day of the month of Adar, in the sixth year of King Darius. That puts it at roughly 516 BC, about seventy years after the original temple was destroyed.

The author of Ezra pauses here to make sure you see who was really behind this. He writes that the people "finished building the temple according to the command of the God of Israel and the decrees of Cyrus, Darius, and Artaxerxes, kings of Persia." Notice the order. The command of God comes first. The decrees of kings come second. The Persian emperors thought they were the ones making decisions. But behind every royal decree, there was a divine command that came first.

The dedication was joyful. They sacrificed bulls, rams, and lambs. They appointed priests and Levites to serve in the temple "as it is written in the book of Moses." And then, just a few weeks later, they celebrated the Passover together for the first time since the return.

The Passover. The meal that remembered how God had rescued his people from Egypt, how the blood of a lamb had saved them from death, how God had led them out of slavery and into freedom. And now, on the other side of a different kind of exodus, they ate it again. They were home. The temple was standing. God had brought them through.

The text says "the Lord had filled them with joy." After the fear, the opposition, the sixteen years of silence, the investigations, and the threats, God filled them with joy. Not just happiness. Joy. The kind that comes from watching God do what he said he would do, despite every obstacle.

WHAT THIS MEANS FOR US

First, worship comes before everything else. The exiles built the altar before they built the temple. They got the priorities right. In your own life, the most important thing isn't your grades, your friendships, or your plans for the future. The most important thing is your relationship with God. Everything else gets built on that foundation.

Second, opposition is normal. Whenever God's people try to do something that matters, resistance shows up. It might be direct and obvious, like the enemies in Ezra. Or it might be subtle, like the slow drift into comfort and distraction that kept the temple unfinished for sixteen years. Either way, expect it. Don't be surprised when doing the right thing gets hard.

Third, it's never too late to start again. The people gave up for sixteen years. Sixteen years! But when the prophets spoke and God stirred their hearts again, they picked up where they left off. If you've dropped something important, if you've let a commitment die or a relationship fade, you can start again. God is in the business of restarts.

Fourth, God uses setbacks for his purposes. Tattenai's investigation looked like disaster. It turned out to be the best thing that could have happened, because it led Darius to confirm and expand the original decree. The thing that threatened to destroy the work ended up guaranteeing it. God has a habit of doing that.

Fifth, God finishes what he starts. The temple got built. Not because the people were perfectly faithful. They weren't. They quit for sixteen years. But God didn't quit. He sent prophets. He moved kings. He watched over his people. And his purposes were accomplished, not because of human perfection, but because of divine persistence.

TALKING POINTS

1. **The exiles built the altar before they built the temple, putting worship first even before the building was finished.** What does it look like to put worship first in your own life, even when other things feel more urgent?

2. **The older generation wept when they saw the new foundation because it didn't compare to what they remembered.**

The younger generation shouted for joy. Why do you think both responses existed at the same time? Have you ever experienced a mix of joy and sadness about the same situation?

3. **The work on the temple stopped for sixteen years because of fear and distraction.** What kinds of things cause you to lose motivation for things that matter? How can you recognize when you've drifted?

4. **When Tattenai investigated the building project, the Jews didn't panic. They calmly explained their history and their authorization.** What gave them confidence to stand firm this time when fear had stopped them before? What had changed?

5. **The Passover celebration at the end of this section reminded the people of God's rescue from Egypt.** Why do you think remembering what God has done in the past helps us trust him for the future?

The temple is standing. The sacrifices are burning. The Passover has been celebrated. But the story of Ezra isn't over. Decades will pass before the next chapter begins, and when it does, the problem won't be enemy armies or hostile neighbors. It will be something much closer to home.

Turn the page.

3

THE MAN WHO TORE HIS ROBES

Mark Twain's *The Prince and the Pauper* tells the story of a young prince who discovers the truth about his own kingdom. Prince Edward of England has grown up inside the palace walls. He's educated, privileged, and surrounded by people who tell him what he wants to hear. He knows he'll be king one day. He assumes his kingdom is basically fine.

Then, through a twist of fate, he ends up on the streets of London dressed in a beggar's rags, and he sees what nobody in the palace ever showed him: the cruelty, the poverty, the injustice, and the suffering of his own people. The laws he thought were fair are crushing the weak. The officials he trusted are corrupt. The kingdom he believed was thriving is rotting from the inside.

Edward is shattered. Not because the problems are happening to him personally, but because they're happening under his name, in his kingdom, on his watch. And when he finally returns to power, he's a different kind of ruler. He can't unsee what he saw. The truth about his kingdom changed him.

That's almost exactly what happens to Ezra. A man who has spent his life studying God's law leaves the comfort of the Persian court and travels hundreds of miles to Jerusalem, expecting to find a community that's faithfully following the Scriptures. After all, the temple has been rebuilt. The sacrifices are burning. The festivals are being celebrated. Everything should be fine.

But when Ezra arrives and sees the truth, what he discovers doesn't just disappoint him. It destroys him. And his response, one of the rawest moments of grief in the entire Bible, will become the thing that changes everything.

FIFTY-EIGHT YEARS LATER

Before we get to the crisis, we need to meet the man at the center of it. Between Ezra 6 and Ezra 7, roughly fifty-eight years pass. The temple was completed in 516 BC. Ezra doesn't arrive in Jerusalem until 458 BC. That's a gap of almost six decades, and the book simply skips over it. During those silent years, the events of the book of Esther took place in Persia, and life in Jerusalem settled into a quiet routine.

Then Ezra steps onto the page, and he's one of the most impressive people in the Bible. The text introduces him with a genealogy that traces his ancestry all the way back to Aaron, the very first high priest. Ezra wasn't just any priest. He had a pedigree that stretched back to the beginning of Israel's worship.

But what made Ezra truly remarkable wasn't his family tree. It was his relationship with Scripture. Ezra 7:10 gives us one of the most important verses in the book: "Ezra had devoted himself to the study and observance of the Law of the Lord, and to teaching its decrees and laws in Israel."

Three things, in that order. He studied it. He obeyed it. He taught it. Ezra didn't just know God's word as an academic exercise. He lived it first, and then he passed it on to others. That combination of knowledge, obedience, and teaching made him exactly the leader this community needed.

King Artaxerxes of Persia gave Ezra an extraordinary commission. He authorized Ezra to lead a group of exiles back to Jerusalem, carry a massive amount of gold and silver for the temple, and establish the Law of Moses as the governing standard for the Jewish community. The king even gave Ezra authority to appoint judges and enforce the law. A pagan king was funding and authorizing the spread of God's word. Once again, just like Cyrus before him, a foreign ruler was being used by God to accomplish divine purposes.

A JOURNEY OF FAITH

Ezra gathered about 1,500 men, plus their families, for the journey. When he assembled the group at a staging area by the Ahava Canal, he noticed a problem: there were no Levites among them. The Levites were essential for temple service, but apparently none had volunteered for the trip. Most of them had built comfortable lives in Babylon and weren't eager to give that up for hard work in Jerusalem. Ezra sent messengers to recruit some, and eventually about thirty-eight Levites agreed to come.

Then Ezra did something that reveals the depth of his faith, and his willingness to put that faith on the line.

He called a fast. The journey from Babylon to Jerusalem was about eight hundred miles through dangerous territory.

Bandits roamed the roads. And Ezra's caravan was carrying a fortune in gold and silver, roughly twenty-five tons of precious metal and objects. They were an obvious target.

Ezra could have asked the king for a military escort. Artaxerxes would have gladly provided soldiers and horsemen. But Ezra had already told the king, "The gracious hand of our God is on everyone who looks to him, but his great anger is against all who forsake him." Having made that bold claim about God's protection, Ezra was too ashamed to turn around and ask for an army. It would have made his faith look hollow.

So instead of soldiers, Ezra called the people to fast and pray. He humbled himself before God and asked for safe passage. And God answered. The text says simply, "The hand of our God was on us, and he protected us from enemies and bandits along the way."

That phrase, "the hand of our God," shows up again and again in these chapters. It's the quiet drumbeat underneath every event. God's hand was on Ezra when the king granted his request. God's hand was on the travelers as they journeyed. God's hand protected the treasure. Ezra didn't see miracles like Moses did, no pillars of fire or parting seas. But he recognized the steady, invisible hand of God guiding everything.

After four months of travel, they arrived safely in Jerusalem with every ounce of gold and silver accounted for.

THE REPORT THAT CHANGED EVERYTHING

Ezra had been in Jerusalem for only a few months when the leaders of the community came to him with devastating news. "The people of Israel, including the priests and the Levites, have not kept themselves separate from the neighboring peoples with their detestable practices. They have taken some of their daughters as wives for themselves and their sons, and have mingled the holy race with the peoples around them. And the leaders and officials have led the way in this unfaithfulness."

Let's pause here, because this is the part that often confuses modern readers. Why was intermarriage such a big deal? Was this about racism? Was God saying that one ethnic group was better than another?

No. The issue was never ethnicity. It was worship.

God had specifically commanded Israel not to intermarry with the surrounding nations, and he gave the reason clearly in Deuteronomy 7:3–4: "Do not intermarry with them… for they will turn your children away from following me to serve other gods." The problem wasn't the nationality of these women. The problem was their gods. History had proven this over and over. Solomon, the wisest man who ever lived, had married foreign women, and they turned his heart away from God (1 Kings 11:1–4). The entire northern kingdom of Israel had been destroyed because of idolatry that crept in through exactly this kind of religious mixing.

The returned exiles were supposed to be a fresh start. They had come back from exile, rebuilt the temple, and recommitted themselves to God. But now, barely a generation later, they were repeating the exact pattern that had gotten their ancestors sent into exile in the first place. And it wasn't just ordinary citizens doing it. The priests and Levites, the very people responsible for leading the community in faithfulness, were among the worst offenders.

The community looked healthy on the outside. The temple was standing. The sacrifices were being offered. But underneath the surface, the foundation was cracking.

EZRA FALLS APART

When Ezra heard the report, he didn't call a meeting. He didn't deliver a lecture. He didn't fire off angry accusations.

He tore his robe and his cloak. He pulled hair from his head and beard. And then he sat down on the ground, stunned, and didn't move until the evening sacrifice.

This was not a performance. This was a man so shattered by what he had heard that he physically fell apart. In the ancient world, tearing your clothes was the most extreme expression of grief and horror. Pulling out your own hair was even beyond that. Ezra was showing, in the most visceral way possible, that this sin wasn't just a policy violation. It was a catastrophe.

And notice something critical: Ezra himself hadn't married a foreign woman. He wasn't personally guilty. But he didn't distance himself from the sin. When he finally prayed, he didn't say "they have sinned." He said "we have sinned." He identified with his people, took their failure onto himself, and brought it before God as if it were his own.

His prayer is one of the rawest, most honest prayers in the Bible. He rehearsed the history of Israel's rebellion, acknowledged that the exile had been deserved, marveled that God had shown mercy by allowing them to return, and then confessed that they were blowing it all over again. He didn't make excuses. He didn't ask for a lighter sentence. He simply laid out the truth before God and threw himself on divine mercy.

"Here we are before you in our guilt," he prayed, "though because of it not one of us can stand in your presence."

That's it. No request. No negotiation. Just a broken man telling the truth to a holy God.

THE PEOPLE RESPOND

While Ezra was praying and weeping on the ground in front of the temple, something remarkable happened. A crowd gathered around him. Men, women, and children. And they started weeping too.

Ezra's grief was contagious. His brokenness over sin created space for other people to feel their own brokenness. A man named Shekaniah stepped forward and said the words that would change everything: "We have been unfaithful to our God by marrying foreign women from the peoples around us. But in spite of this, there is still hope for Israel."

Still hope. Even now. Even after this.

Shekaniah proposed a solution: the community would make a covenant before God to send away the foreign wives and their children, in accordance with God's law. It was a radical, painful, gut-wrenching proposal. But the people agreed. They called a nationwide assembly. Within three days, every man in Judah and Benjamin gathered in the open square before the temple, shivering in the December rain, distressed by the occasion and the cold.

Ezra stood before them and spoke plainly: "You have been unfaithful. You have married foreign women, adding to Israel's guilt. Now honor the Lord, the God of your ancestors, and do his will."

The people answered with one voice: "You are right. We must do as you say."

THE PAINFUL RESOLUTION

The process took three months. Family by family, case by case, a council of leaders investigated every intermarriage and worked through the separations. The book lists the names of those found guilty, starting with the priests and Levites. That's not an accident. The Bible doesn't hide the failures of its leaders. It puts them right at the top of the list.

This is, without question, one of the most uncomfortable passages in the Bible. The human cost was enormous. Wives were sent away. Children were affected. Families were torn apart. The text doesn't soften this or pretend it was easy. It simply records what happened and moves on.

Was this the right thing to do? Was it the only option? The text doesn't invite us to celebrate it. What it does is show us how seriously God takes faithfulness, and how devastating the consequences of compromise can be. The community had to choose between comfort and covenant, between keeping things as they were and returning to what God had called them to be. They chose the harder path. And the book of Ezra ends there, on that painful, unresolved note, a people in the middle of a reckoning that had no easy answers.

But remember Shekaniah's words: "There is still hope for Israel." That's the thread the whole Bible is pulling on. Even when God's people fail, even when the situation looks hopeless, God's grace is stubborn enough to keep working.

WHAT THIS MEANS FOR US

First, what you do with God's word defines your life. Ezra studied it, obeyed it, and taught it. That three-part pattern changed a nation. Your relationship with the Bible isn't just about reading. It's about letting it shape how you actually live, and then helping others do the same.

Second, real faith gets tested. Ezra could have taken the king's soldiers. It would have been the safe, reasonable thing to do. Instead, he put his faith where his mouth was. Sometimes following God means choosing the harder path specifically because it forces you to depend on him.

Third, sin doesn't stay contained. The intermarriage problem didn't happen overnight. It crept in gradually, one compromise at a time, until it had reached the highest levels of leadership. Sin works the same way in our lives. Small choices that seem harmless can quietly erode the things that matter most. Pay attention to the small compromises before they become big ones.

Fourth, godly leaders grieve before they fix. Ezra's first response to the crisis wasn't a plan of action. It was prayer and tears. He didn't rush to judgment or condemnation. He sat in the grief of it, identified with the sin of his people, and brought it to God. There's a lesson there for anyone who sees something wrong in the world: mourn it before you try to fix it. Pray about it before you preach about it.

Fifth, there is always hope. The situation in Ezra 9–10 looked terrible. The very community that was supposed to represent a fresh start was repeating old mistakes. But Shekaniah's words cut through the despair: "There is still hope." That's true for Israel, and it's true for you. No matter how badly you've failed, no matter how far you've drifted, God's mercy is bigger than your mess.

TALKING POINTS

1. **Ezra 7:10 says Ezra devoted himself to studying, obeying, and teaching God's law, in that order.** Why do you think the order matters? What happens when someone tries to teach something they haven't first lived?

2. **Ezra refused the king's military escort because he had already told the king that God would protect them.** Have you ever been in a situation where you had to back up your words about God with your actions? What did that feel like?

3. **The intermarriage crisis wasn't about ethnicity but about worship.** How can relationships and friendships pull us away from faithfulness to God? How do you know when a relationship is helping or hurting your walk with God?

4. **Ezra didn't personally commit the sin he was grieving over, but he prayed "we have sinned" instead of "they have sinned."** What does it look like to take responsibility for the failures of your community or your family, not just your own individual mistakes?

5. **The book of Ezra ends on a painful, unresolved note. There are no trumpets or celebrations.** Why do you think the book ends this way? What does it tell us about the ongoing struggle between human failure and God's faithfulness?

The book of Ezra closes with a community in the middle of a painful reformation, a people trying to get right with God after discovering how far they had drifted. But the story doesn't end here. Years will pass. The walls of Jerusalem will still lie in ruins. And one day, in a Persian palace far from Judah, a man named Nehemiah will hear the news that breaks his heart and sets him on a journey that will change everything.

Turn the page.

4

THE CUPBEARER AND THE KING

There's a scene in Disney's *One Hundred and One Dalmatians* that changes the entire movie. Pongo and Perdita are at home when they learn the terrible news: their fifteen puppies have been stolen. Cruella de Vil has taken them to a remote estate, and she plans to destroy them. The situation is desperate, and no human seems able to help.

So Pongo does something extraordinary. He goes to the window and launches the "Twilight Bark," a chain of communication that spreads across all of London and into the countryside—dog to dog, farm to farm—until the message reaches two animals near the estate where the puppies are being held. What follows is one of the great rescue missions in animated film. Pongo and Perdita brave a freezing winter night, outsmart Cruella's henchmen, and lead not just their own fifteen puppies but eighty-four others to safety. The whole operation depends on hearing the right news at the right time, making a bold plan, and then having the courage to carry it out.

Nehemiah's story begins the same way: with devastating news that demands a response. A man who had every reason to stay comfortable in a palace hears about a crisis far away and decides he can't do nothing. What follows is one of the most impressive displays of prayer, strategy, and courage in the entire Bible.

NEWS FROM HOME

Nehemiah was living in Susa, the winter capital of the Persian Empire, in roughly 445 BC. He held one of the most trusted positions in the ancient world: he was the cupbearer to King Artaxerxes. That might not sound impressive at first, but the cupbearer wasn't just someone who poured drinks. He was the person who tasted the king's wine to prove it wasn't poisoned. That meant the king trusted him with his life. It also meant Nehemiah had regular, personal access to the most powerful man on earth.

By all appearances, Nehemiah had it made. He had a high-ranking position, job security, and the ear of the king. He was hundreds of miles from the struggles of Jerusalem. He could have lived out his days in comfort and never thought twice about the little community back in Judah.

But then his brother Hanani arrived from Jerusalem with a group of other men. Nehemiah asked them how things were going back home, and the answer hit him like a punch to the stomach.

"Those who survived the exile and are back in the province are in great trouble and disgrace. The wall of Jerusalem is broken down, and its gates have been burned with fire."

This wasn't ancient history. This was fresh devastation. The walls that may have been partially rebuilt had been torn down again, likely by enemies who had convinced the Persian authorities that Jerusalem was a threat. The gates were ashes. The city that was supposed to be "the joy of the whole earth" was exposed, defenseless, and humiliated. Anyone who wanted to attack the people inside could simply walk in.

For Nehemiah, this wasn't just political news. This was personal. Jerusalem was his ancestral home. These were his people. And the condition of the city was a disgrace not just to them but to the God they served. What would the surrounding nations think about a God whose own city lay in ruins?

A PRAYER THAT LASTED FOUR MONTHS

When Nehemiah heard the report, he sat down and wept. Then he did something that most people in his position would not have done. He didn't immediately start making plans. He didn't rush to the king with a request. He didn't send angry letters or organize a committee.

He prayed. For four months.

That's not a typo. Nehemiah received the news in the month of Kislev (roughly November/December) and didn't approach the king until the month of Nisan (roughly March/April). For four solid months, he fasted, mourned, and prayed before the God of heaven.

His prayer, recorded in Nehemiah 1:5–11, is a masterclass in how to talk to God. He started with worship, acknowledging who God is: "the great and awesome God, who keeps his covenant of love with those who love him and obey his commands." He didn't open with his problem. He opened with God's character. That matters, because the size of your problem depends on the size of your God. If God is small, the broken walls are insurmountable. If God is great and awesome and covenant-keeping, then broken walls are something he can handle.

Then Nehemiah confessed sin. Not just the sins of the people in Jerusalem, not just the sins of previous generations, but his own. "I confess the sins we Israelites, including myself and my father's house, have committed against you." Like Ezra before him, Nehemiah didn't separate himself from the community's failure. He owned it.

Then he reminded God of his promises. He quoted Scripture back to God, drawing on passages from Deuteronomy where God had said that if his scattered people returned to him, he would gather them and bring them back. Nehemiah was essentially saying, "God, you promised this. Your word is on the line. Act on what you said."

And finally, at the very end, Nehemiah made his specific request: "Give your servant success today by granting him favor in the presence of this man."

This man. That's how Nehemiah referred to the king of the Persian Empire. Not "this mighty ruler" or "this terrifying monarch." This man. Because in Nehemiah's mind, Artaxerxes was powerful, but he was still just a man under the authority of the God of heaven.

Then Nehemiah dropped a detail he had been saving: "I was cupbearer to the king." The reader suddenly realizes that Nehemiah isn't just some exile praying from a distance. He's standing inside the palace. He has access. God has already positioned him exactly where he needs to be.

THE MOST DANGEROUS CONVERSATION OF HIS LIFE

Four months of prayer led to one moment. Nehemiah was serving wine to the king when Artaxerxes noticed something was wrong. "Why does your face look so sad when you are not ill? This can be nothing but sadness of heart."

Nehemiah was terrified. In the Persian court, showing sadness in the king's presence was risky. The king might take it as an insult or, worse, suspect a plot. Servants were expected to be cheerful and invisible. A gloomy face could get you removed from your position or even killed.

But Nehemiah had been praying for this moment for four months. He answered carefully, respectfully, and strategically. He didn't mention Jerusalem by name, at least not right away. Instead, he framed it personally: "Why should my face not look sad when the city where my fathers are buried lies in ruins, and its gates have been destroyed by fire?" He appealed to the king's sympathy first, not his politics.

The king asked the critical question: "What is it you want?"

And right there, in the space between that question and his answer, Nehemiah prayed. Not a long prayer. Not even an audible one, probably. Just a quick, silent cry to the God of heaven. The text says simply, "Then I prayed to the God of heaven, and I answered the king."

This is one of the great moments in the Bible. Months of deep, sustained prayer had prepared Nehemiah for this instant. The quick prayer in the moment wasn't a substitute for the long prayers that came before. It was the fruit of them. Because Nehemiah had spent four months in conversation with God, he was ready when the thirty-second window opened.

He made his request. He asked to be sent to Jerusalem to rebuild it. And because he had planned carefully during those months of prayer, he didn't stop with a vague appeal. He asked for specific things: letters of safe conduct to the governors along the route, and a letter to the keeper of the king's forest for timber to build the gates and walls.

The king granted every request. Nehemiah knew exactly why: "because the gracious hand of my God was upon me."

ARRIVAL AND OPPOSITION

Unlike Ezra, who had refused a military escort because he had boasted to the king about God's protection, Nehemiah accepted one. This wasn't a lack of faith. It was a different personality and a different situation. The military escort made a statement: the king's policy toward Jerusalem had officially changed. Nehemiah arrived with authority, and everyone who saw the soldiers knew it.

But not everyone was pleased. Two men in particular were deeply disturbed by Nehemiah's arrival: Sanballat the Horonite and Tobiah the Ammonite official. These were powerful men with political influence in the region. Sanballat was likely the governor of Samaria, and Tobiah was a well-connected official in Ammon. A third enemy, Geshem the Arab, controlled a confederation of tribes to the south. Together, these three essentially surrounded Judah from every direction.

They were troubled, the text says, because "someone had come to promote the welfare of the Israelites." That sentence reveals everything about their motives. They didn't oppose Nehemiah because he was doing something wrong. They opposed him because he was doing something good, and good things for Jerusalem were bad things for their power.

THE MIDNIGHT SURVEY

Nehemiah arrived in Jerusalem and rested for three days. Then, in the middle of the night, he did something no one expected.

He got on a horse and rode out to inspect the walls. He told no one what God had put in his heart to do. He took only a few men with him. No officials, no priests, no leaders. Just Nehemiah and a handful of trusted companions, picking their way through rubble in the dark.

He started at the Valley Gate on the west side and moved south toward the Dung Gate, then east to the Fountain Gate and the King's Pool. At some point the debris was so thick that his horse couldn't get through, and he had to continue on foot along the valley. He saw the full extent of the damage: collapsed walls, burned gates, piles of stone so massive they blocked the roads.

Why the secrecy? Because Nehemiah was a planner. He didn't want to announce a project before he understood the scope of it. He didn't want the enemies to know what he was thinking before he was ready. And he didn't want the people's first encounter with the plan to be a half-formed idea that could be shot down by doubt or fear. He wanted to see the problem with his own eyes, form a plan, and then present it with confidence.

This is leadership. Not just vision, but preparation. Not just passion, but strategy.

"LET US START REBUILDING"

When Nehemiah was ready, he called the leaders together and laid it out. He didn't sugarcoat the problem: "You see the trouble we are in. Jerusalem lies in ruins, and its gates have been burned with fire." He identified with them, using the word "we," not "you." Their disgrace was his disgrace.

Then he shared the solution: "Come, let us rebuild the wall of Jerusalem, and we will no longer be in disgrace."

And then he played his strongest card. He told them about the hand of God on his life, how the king had granted every request, how the letters and the timber and the military escort had all come together in ways that could only be explained by divine provision. He laid the evidence before them and let them draw the obvious conclusion: God was in this.

The response was immediate: "Let us start rebuilding." And they began the work.

Of course, the enemies responded too. Sanballat, Tobiah, and Geshem heard about the plan and immediately began mocking and threatening: "What is this you are doing? Are you rebelling against the king?"

It was the same old accusation. The same lie that had shut down the building project before. They were hoping fear would work again.

But Nehemiah was not Zerubbabel's generation. He had the king's letters. He had the hand of God. And he had the spine to say what needed to be said: "The God of heaven will give us success. We his servants will start rebuilding, but as for you, you have no share in Jerusalem or any claim or historic right to it."

No negotiation. No compromise. No fear. Just a man who had prayed for four months, planned with precision, and was now ready to build.

WHAT THIS MEANS FOR US

First, position is often preparation. Nehemiah didn't end up as cupbearer to the king by accident. God placed him there years before the crisis happened. Sometimes the job you have, the school you're at, or the neighborhood you live in isn't random. God may be positioning you for something you can't see yet.

Second, prayer and planning go together. Nehemiah didn't choose between praying and planning. He did both. Four months of prayer produced a plan so detailed that he knew exactly what to ask the king for. Prayer without planning can become an excuse for passivity. Planning without prayer can become arrogance. Nehemiah shows us what it looks like to combine them.

Third, long preparation produces short-window readiness. The arrow prayer in Nehemiah 2:4 took about two seconds. But it was built on four months of sustained prayer. When your moment comes, whether it's a conversation, a decision, or an opportunity, you won't have time to prepare from scratch. The preparation has to happen beforehand. The people who are ready for critical moments are the people who have been praying before those moments arrive.

Fourth, real leaders identify with the problem. Nehemiah didn't say "you have a problem." He said "we are in trouble." He didn't stand above the people and give orders. He stood with them and shared their disgrace. That's why they followed him. People don't follow leaders who look down on them. They follow leaders who stand beside them.

Fifth, opposition is a sign you're doing something that matters. Sanballat and Tobiah didn't show up because Nehemiah was wasting his time. They showed up because he was threatening their power by doing something genuinely good. If nobody opposes what you're doing, it might be because it isn't important enough to oppose.

TALKING POINTS

1. **Nehemiah held a powerful position in the Persian court but couldn't ignore the crisis in Jerusalem.** Have you ever been comfortable in one area of your life but felt pulled to care about a problem somewhere else? What did you do about it?

2. **Nehemiah prayed for four months before he acted.** Why do you think he waited so long? What's the difference between waiting on God and just procrastinating? How can you tell which one you're doing?

3. **When the king asked "What is it you want?", Nehemiah shot a quick prayer to God before answering.** What does that tell us about his relationship with God? How can someone develop the kind of connection where prayer becomes instinctive, not just something you do at bedtime?

4. **Nehemiah surveyed the walls secretly at night before telling anyone his plan.** What does this teach us about the importance of preparation before going public with an idea? Have you ever shared a plan too early and had it fall apart?

5. **Nehemiah's enemies tried to discourage the work through mockery and accusations.** What forms does that

kind of opposition take in your life? How do you decide when to respond and when to ignore it?

The walls are a wreck. The enemies are circling. The people have said yes, but the work hasn't started yet. And when it does, the opposition won't just mock from a distance. It will get personal, get physical, and get dangerous.

Turn the page.

5

SWORDS AND TROWELS

Johann David Wyss' *The Swiss Family Robinson* opens with a disaster. A family of six is shipwrecked on an uninhabited island with no rescue in sight. They have nothing but what they can salvage from the wreck and what the island provides. Their survival depends on one thing: everyone working together.

And they do. The father engineers shelters and tools. The mother organizes supplies and keeps the family fed. Each of the four sons takes on tasks suited to their abilities. One hunts. One builds. One explores. One tends animals. They construct a treehouse, a bridge, a garden, a fortified shelter. They face threats from wild animals, storms, and the constant pressure of the unknown. But through it all, the family survives because every member contributes, and nobody sits on the sideline waiting to be rescued.

That's a picture of what happens in Nehemiah 3–7. A community surrounded by enemies, working against the clock, builds an entire city wall in less than two months. Priests lay bricks. Goldsmiths mix mortar. Perfume-makers haul stones. Fathers build next to their daughters. Government officials pick up shovels. At one point, half the workers hold weapons while the other half builds, and the builders themselves carry swords on their belts while they work.

It's one of the most dramatic construction projects in history. And it almost didn't happen.

EVERYONE BUILDS

Nehemiah 3 is one of those chapters people tend to skip. It's a long list of names, sections of wall, and gates, going all the way around Jerusalem from the Sheep Gate in the north back to the Sheep Gate again. If you read it quickly, it just looks like a construction log.

But slow down and look at who's actually doing the work.

The high priest Eliashib and his fellow priests start things off by rebuilding the Sheep Gate. The leader of half the district of Jerusalem works on another section. Goldsmiths and perfume-makers, people whose regular jobs involved delicate, indoor work, are out in the sun hauling rubble. One official rebuilds a section with the help of his daughters. Merchants repair the stretch near their shops. Priests fix the portions of wall near their own homes.

That last detail is important. Many of the builders worked on the section of wall closest to where they lived. The logic was simple and brilliant: you'll fight hardest to protect the wall that protects your own family. Nehemiah understood that the best motivation isn't guilt or obligation. It's personal investment.

The list also reveals something uncomfortable. Buried in verse 5 is this note: "The next section was repaired by the men of Tekoa, but their nobles would not put their shoulders to the work under their supervisors." The nobles of Tekoa refused to help. They were too important, too proud, too comfortable to do manual labor alongside commoners. While priests and perfume-makers and merchants' daughters were getting their hands dirty, these wealthy leaders wouldn't stoop.

The text doesn't editorialize. It doesn't say "and God punished them." It just records their refusal and moves on. But their names are conspicuously absent from a chapter full of people being honored for their contribution. Meanwhile, the regular people of Tekoa cared so much that they rebuilt two separate sections, as if to make up for what their leaders wouldn't do.

That one verse tells you a lot about what God values. It's not your title that matters. It's whether you showed up.

MOCKERY

The enemies wasted no time. Sanballat was furious when he heard the building had started. He gathered an audience of officials and soldiers and launched into a string of mocking questions: "What are those feeble Jews doing? Will they restore their wall? Will they offer sacrifices? Will they finish in a day? Can they bring the stones back to life from those heaps of rubble?"

His sidekick Tobiah piled on: "What they are building, even a fox climbing up on it would break down their stone wall!"

This was calculated mockery, designed not just to entertain Sanballat's supporters but to filter back to the builders and break their spirit. Ridicule is one of the oldest weapons in the world, and it doesn't need any facts to be effective. You don't have to prove someone is wrong. You just have to make them feel foolish enough to quit.

Nehemiah's response? He prayed. Not a polite, measured prayer either. He poured out his frustration to God, asking him to deal with the insults. Then, without missing a beat, the text says: "So we built the wall."

That sentence is one of the great understatements in the Bible. After all the mockery and intimidation, the response was just… they kept building. They got the wall to half its intended height because, the text says, "the people worked with all their heart."

Ridicule works when people are unsure of their purpose. It crumbles against people who know exactly what they're doing and why.

THE RING TIGHTENS

When mockery didn't work, the enemies escalated. Sanballat formed an alliance with the Ammonites, the Arabs, and the people of Ashdod. They now surrounded Jerusalem from every direction: north, south, east, and west. And they began plotting an actual attack.

Inside Jerusalem, things weren't much better. The workers were exhausted. A gloomy saying started making the rounds: "The strength of the laborers is giving out, and there is so much rubble that we cannot rebuild the wall." Outside, the enemies kept saying, "Before they know it or see us, we will be right there among them and will kill them and put an end to the work."

Fear was doing what mockery couldn't: it was eroding the people from the inside.

Nehemiah responded with a move that was half military strategy and half sermon. He stationed armed guards at the most vulnerable points of the wall and organized the workers by families, so brothers and fathers and sons stood together. Then he addressed the crowd: "Don't be afraid of them. Remember the Lord, who is great and awesome, and fight for your families, your sons and your daughters, your wives and your homes."

Remember the Lord, and fight. Not one or the other. Both.

When the enemies realized their surprise attack had been discovered and their plans exposed, they backed off. But Nehemiah didn't relax. From that point on, the construction site became a military operation. Half the men worked while the other half stood guard with spears, shields, and bows. The builders carried swords at their belts. The carriers held weapons in one hand and supplies in the other. A trumpeter stood beside Nehemiah at all times, ready to sound the alarm if any section came under attack.

Nehemiah told the people, "The work is extensive and spread out, and we are widely separated from each other along the wall. Wherever you hear the sound of the trumpet, join us there. Our God will fight for us."

They didn't even change their clothes at night. They slept in them, weapons within reach, ready for whatever came.

THE ENEMY WITHIN

Then came a threat Nehemiah didn't see coming, and it didn't come from Sanballat. It came from inside the community.

The poorer families were running out of food. The wall-building project meant they couldn't tend their fields.

Some had mortgaged their land just to eat. Others had borrowed money to pay the Persian taxes. And the wealthy members of the community were charging interest on the loans, seizing property, and even taking children as slaves when families couldn't pay. Jewish brothers were exploiting Jewish brothers.

The women raised the outcry. They were the ones watching their children go hungry while their husbands worked on the wall all day. The text says it was "a great outcry," the kind of cry that comes from desperate people with nothing left to lose.

Nehemiah was furious. He called a public assembly and confronted the wealthy leaders to their faces: "What you are doing is not right. We bought back our Jewish brothers who were sold to the Gentiles, and now you are selling your own brothers?" The accused had nothing to say in their defense. Nehemiah demanded that they return the fields, vineyards, and houses they had taken, and refund the interest they had charged. They agreed.

Then Nehemiah shook out the folds of his robe and said, "In this way may God shake out of their house and possessions anyone who does not keep this promise." The whole assembly said "Amen" and did as they had promised.

What makes this episode so striking is that Nehemiah could have ignored it. He was focused on the wall. The external enemies were dangerous enough. Dealing with internal corruption was messy and politically risky. But Nehemiah understood something crucial: a wall can protect you from enemies outside, but it can't protect you from injustice inside. A community that exploits its own members isn't worth defending.

He also led by example. For twelve years as governor, Nehemiah never took the food allowance that was his right. Previous governors had taxed the people heavily to fund their own lifestyles, but Nehemiah paid for everything, including feeding 150 people at his table every day, out of his own resources. "I did not do this," he said, "because of the fear of God."

THE FINAL SCHEMES

As the wall neared completion, Sanballat grew desperate. He tried four more tactics in rapid succession.

First, he invited Nehemiah to a meeting on the plain of Ono, about a day's journey from Jerusalem. It was almost certainly a trap. Nehemiah's reply was blunt: "I am carrying on a great project and cannot go down. Why should the work stop while I leave it and go down to you?" Sanballat sent this invitation four times. Nehemiah refused four times.

Second, Sanballat sent an open letter, meaning everyone could read it, accusing Nehemiah of planning a rebellion against Persia and setting himself up as king. It was a lie designed to create panic and force Nehemiah to come negotiate. Nehemiah's response: "Nothing like what you are saying is happening; you are just making it up out of your head."

Third, a man named Shemaiah, who was probably a prophet, told Nehemiah that assassins were coming to kill him that night and that he should hide inside the temple to save his life. It sounded like a warning from a friend. But Nehemiah saw through it. Going into the temple would have been cowardly and illegal, since Nehemiah was not a priest and had no right to enter. It would have ruined his reputation and demoralized the workers. "Should a man like me run away?" Nehemiah answered. "Should someone like me go into the temple to save his life? I will not go!" He later realized Shemaiah had been hired by Tobiah and Sanballat to discredit him.

Fourth, Tobiah had allies inside Jerusalem who constantly praised him to Nehemiah and reported Nehemiah's private words back to Tobiah. The community was riddled with divided loyalties. Nehemiah couldn't trust everyone around him.

Through all of it, mockery, threats, lies, traps, bribery, espionage, internal corruption, and exhaustion, Nehemiah held the line.

FIFTY-TWO DAYS

"So the wall was completed on the twenty-fifth of Elul, in fifty-two days." That's it. One sentence. After five chapters of drama, danger, and near disaster, the text announces the completion of the wall with the same understated calm it always uses for God's greatest accomplishments.

Fifty-two days. Less than two months. A wall that the enemies said couldn't be built, that a fox could knock down, that would never be finished, was standing around the entire city.

The surrounding nations noticed. The text says "they were afraid and lost their self-confidence, because they realized that this work had been done with the help of our God." Even the enemies could see it. This wasn't just human effort. Something bigger was at work.

After the wall was complete, Nehemiah turned his attention to the community itself. He appointed his brother Hanani and a man named Hananiah to govern the city. He organized guards at the gates. And then he did something that connected this moment to the very beginning of the story: he found the genealogical list of the first exiles who had returned under Zerubbabel decades earlier. The same list that appears in Ezra 2. He wanted to make sure this community knew who they were and where they came from.

The wall was up. But Nehemiah knew that stones and gates don't make a people. Identity does. Faithfulness does. And the hardest work was still ahead.

WHAT THIS MEANS FOR US

First, everyone has a role. The building list in Nehemiah 3 includes priests, politicians, perfume-makers, goldsmiths, merchants, and daughters. Nobody was too important or too unimportant to contribute. In God's work, there's no such thing as a spectator. Whatever your abilities are, they're needed.

Second, expect opposition to escalate. The enemies didn't give up after mockery failed. They moved to threats, then plots, then lies, then hired prophets, then internal sabotage. When you're doing something that matters, opposition doesn't just go away. It adapts. Be ready for it to change shape.

Third, internal problems are more dangerous than external enemies. The economic exploitation in chapter 5 nearly tore the community apart from the inside. Sanballat couldn't stop the wall, but greed within the community almost did. Watch for the threats that come from within, not just from outside.

Fourth, leaders lead by example, not just by instruction. Nehemiah didn't just tell people to sacrifice. He sacrificed first. He gave up his governor's salary. He worked on the wall himself. He slept in his clothes. People follow leaders who share the burden, not leaders who just assign it.

Fifth, finishing matters. The wall took fifty-two days. That's impressive, but every one of those days involved a choice to keep going. The people could have quit after the mockery, the threats, the exhaustion, or the internal crisis. They didn't. And because they finished, even their enemies had to admit that God was in it.

TALKING POINTS

1. **Nehemiah 3 lists all kinds of people working on the wall, from priests to goldsmiths to merchants' daughters. But the nobles of Tekoa refused to help.** What do you think made them different from everyone else? What keeps people from pitching in when there's important work to do?

2. **The enemies used mockery as their first weapon.** Why is ridicule so effective at discouraging people? How do you respond when someone makes fun of something you care about?

3. **Nehemiah told the people to "remember the Lord" and also to "fight for your families."** Why did he combine those two things? How do trusting God and taking practical action work together in your own life?

4. **The internal crisis of rich exploiting poor almost destroyed the community from inside.** Why are internal problems often harder to deal with than external ones? Can you think of a time when conflict within a group was more damaging than pressure from outside?

5. **The wall was finished in fifty-two days, and even the enemies recognized that God had helped.** Have you ever

accomplished something that surprised even the people who doubted you? What role did persistence play in getting it done?

The wall is standing. The gates are hung. The city is secured. But Nehemiah knows that walls don't build a nation. People do. And for that, the community will need something it hasn't had in a long time: the word of God, read aloud, explained clearly, and taken to heart. What happens next will be one of the most powerful scenes in the entire Bible.

Turn the page.

6

WHEN THE BOOK WAS OPENED

There's a scene near the end of Disney's *Snow White and the Seven Dwarfs* that's almost too painful to watch. Snow White lies in a glass coffin in the forest. She looks dead. The dwarfs stand around her, hats in their hands, weeping. The forest creatures who once danced with her sit in silence. Nobody speaks. Nobody knows what to do. The girl who filled their home with singing and laughter and life is gone, and as far as anyone can tell, the story is over.

But she isn't dead. She's sleeping. And when the prince arrives and she awakens, the grief of every creature watching flips in an instant to wild, uncontainable joy. The dwarfs who were sobbing moments ago are dancing. The birds are singing. The whole forest erupts because the thing they mourned as lost has come back to life.

That scene kept coming back to me as I studied Nehemiah 8–10. Because here's what happens: the people of Jerusalem gather in an open square to hear the Law of Moses read aloud, many of them hearing it explained clearly for the first time in their lives. And when they understand what it says, they start weeping. The grief is overwhelming. They can see how far they've fallen, how much they've lost, how badly they've failed.

But the leaders tell them to stop crying. Not because the grief isn't real, but because the story isn't over. The law they thought was dead and buried, the ancient festivals they'd forgotten, the covenant promises they'd broken, it's all still there. Still alive. Still waiting to be picked up and lived again. And when the people finally understand this, their weeping turns to celebration so joyful that the text says they went home and "celebrated with great joy, because they now understood the words that had been made known to them."

Something that looked dead woke up. And everything changed.

THE ASSEMBLY

The wall had been finished only days earlier. Fifty-two days of exhausting, dangerous work were behind them. You might expect the people to take a break, catch their breath, maybe throw a party. Instead, they did something nobody forced them to do.

They gathered.

The entire community assembled in the open square before the Water Gate on the east side of the city. Men, women, and every child old enough to understand. Then they did something even more remarkable: they asked Ezra to bring out the Book of the Law of Moses and read it to them. This wasn't a command from Nehemiah. It wasn't on a schedule. The people wanted to hear God's word. The desire came from them.

Ezra stood on a large wooden platform that had been specially built for the occasion, high enough for everyone to see him. Thirteen men stood beside him, some on his right and some on his left. When he opened the scroll, the entire crowd stood to their feet. Ezra blessed the Lord, and the people responded with a thundering "Amen! Amen!" Then they lifted their hands and bowed with their faces to the ground.

He read from early morning until noon. Six hours of Scripture, read aloud, to a crowd standing in the open air. And the text says they "listened attentively."

But reading wasn't enough. Understanding mattered. So while Ezra and others read from the platform, Levites moved through the crowd, explaining the meaning of what was being read. The text describes it carefully: "They read from the Book of the Law of God, making it clear and giving the meaning so that the people could understand what was being read."

This is one of the most important verses in the Bible about the Bible. God's word isn't meant to be merely recited. It's meant to be understood. It's not a magic spell that works automatically. It's a message that transforms people when it gets from the page into their hearts. The Levites made sure that happened. They translated where necessary, explained what was confusing, and helped people connect ancient words to their present lives.

TEARS AND JOY

Then something happened that nobody expected. The people started to weep. As the words of the Law sank in, the crowd was overwhelmed. They heard God's commands and realized how far they had fallen short. They heard his warnings and understood why the exile had happened. They heard his promises and felt the weight of how many they had broken. The conviction was crushing. Tears streamed down faces across the entire assembly.

And then the leaders said something astonishing: "Stop crying."

Nehemiah, Ezra, and the Levites moved through the crowd with the same message: "This day is sacred to the Lord your God. Do not mourn or weep."

That seems strange at first. The people were having a genuine spiritual response. They were convicted of sin. Isn't that exactly what's supposed to happen when you hear God's word? Why would the leaders tell them to stop?

Because conviction wasn't the end of the story. It was the beginning. The point of hearing God's word wasn't to leave the people crushed under the weight of their failures. It was to bring them face to face with a God who is holy but also merciful, who judges but also forgives, who demands obedience but also gives fresh starts. The weeping was appropriate, but it couldn't be the final response. Not today. Today was sacred. And sacred days call for celebration.

Nehemiah told the people, "Go and enjoy choice food and sweet drinks, and send some to those who have nothing prepared. This day is sacred to our Lord. Do not grieve, for the joy of the Lord is your strength."

The joy of the Lord is your strength. That single sentence has echoed through centuries of faith. It doesn't mean "be happy all the time." It means that real strength, the kind that sustains you through hard seasons and honest reckoning, comes not from pretending everything is fine but from knowing that the God who sees your failures is also the God who delights in restoring you. Joy and conviction aren't opposites. They're partners.

The people obeyed. They went home, ate and drank, shared with those who had nothing, and "celebrated with great joy, because they now understood the words that had been made known to them." Understanding changed everything. They didn't just hear the words. They grasped what they meant. And that understanding produced not despair but joy.

A FESTIVAL REDISCOVERED

The next day, the family leaders came back to Ezra for more. They weren't satisfied with a single day of hearing God's word. They wanted to go deeper. And as they studied together, they discovered something they had been missing.

The Law commanded that during the seventh month, the Israelites should celebrate the Feast of Tabernacles by building temporary shelters out of branches and living in them for seven days. It was a reminder of the wilderness years, when God led his people through the desert and they lived in temporary dwellings, entirely dependent on him for food, water, and direction.

The people hadn't celebrated this festival properly in generations. The text makes an extraordinary claim: "From the days of Joshua son of Nun until that day, the Israelites had not celebrated it like this." That's a span of roughly a thousand years. The festival had been observed at various times throughout Israel's history, but never with this level of understanding, this level of community participation, this level of joy.

So the people went out and gathered branches from olive trees, palm trees, and other shade trees. They built shelters on their rooftops, in their courtyards, in the courts of the temple, and in the open squares near the gates. For seven days, the whole community lived in these makeshift structures, reading God's word every day, and celebrating with enormous joy.

There's something beautiful about this image. A people who had just finished building a permanent wall, a symbol of security and strength, immediately moved into temporary shelters, symbols of vulnerability and dependence. The wall said "we are safe." The shelters said "we are still pilgrims who need God every day." Both statements were true. Both needed to be remembered.

THE LONGEST PRAYER

Two days after the festival ended, the people gathered again. But this time the mood was different. They came wearing rough clothing and with dust on their heads, the ancient signs of mourning and repentance. They separated themselves from all foreigners and stood to confess their sins and the sins of their ancestors.

For a quarter of the day they listened to God's word. For another quarter they confessed and worshiped. And then the Levites led the assembly in one of the longest and most sweeping prayers in the entire Bible.

It's a prayer that retells the whole story of Israel from the very beginning. It starts with creation: "You alone are the Lord. You made the heavens, even the highest heavens, and all their starry host, the earth and all that is on it." It moves to Abraham: God chose him, made promises to him, and kept those promises. It covers the exodus: the plagues, the parting of the sea, the pillar of fire and cloud. It recalls Mount Sinai: the giving of the Law, the golden calf, God's patience. It describes the wilderness: manna, water, clothes that didn't wear out for forty years. It covers the conquest of Canaan, the period of the judges, and the long, heartbreaking cycle of rebellion that led to the exile.

And through it all, a pattern emerges. The prayer alternates between two phrases that appear again and again. On one side: "But they were disobedient and rebelled against you." On the other: "But in your great mercy you did not put an end to them or abandon them, for you are a gracious and merciful God."

They sinned. But you forgave. They rebelled. But you were patient. They turned away. But you brought them back. Over and over, century after century, the same rhythm. Human failure met by divine faithfulness. It wasn't that the people's sin didn't matter. It mattered enormously. But God's mercy was always, always bigger.

The prayer ends in the present tense: "But see, we are slaves today, slaves in the land you gave our ancestors." Even after the return from exile, even after the temple was rebuilt and the walls were standing, they were still under Persian rule. The story wasn't over. The full restoration hadn't come yet. They were honest enough to say so.

And yet. They prayed with hope. Because the God they were talking to had a track record. He had never fully abandoned his people, no matter how many times they deserved it.

THE COVENANT RENEWED

The prayer led to action. The people didn't just confess and go home. They made a binding agreement, written down and sealed by their leaders. Nehemiah signed first. Then the priests, the Levites, and the heads of families.

The rest of the people joined in, taking an oath with a curse attached: if they broke the covenant, they were calling down consequences on themselves. It was that serious.

The specific commitments they made were practical and pointed, aimed directly at the failures that had gotten them into trouble before. They promised not to intermarry with the surrounding peoples. They promised to keep the sabbath, refusing to buy or sell on that day even when foreign merchants showed up with goods. They promised to let the land rest every seventh year. They promised to pay a temple tax for the upkeep of worship. They promised to bring their firstfruits, their tithes, and their offerings.

The final sentence of their pledge says it all: "We will not neglect the house of our God." That was the commitment that tied everything together. The temple was the center of their identity as God's people. The sacrifices, the festivals, the daily rhythm of worship, all of it happened there. To neglect the house of God was to neglect God himself. They had done that before the exile, and it had cost them everything. They were determined not to make the same mistake again.

WHAT THIS MEANS FOR US

First, God's word is meant to be understood, not just heard. The Levites didn't just read the scroll and walk away. They explained it. They made it clear. They gave the meaning. If you've ever felt confused by the Bible, that's not a sign of failure. It's a sign that you need help understanding, and that help is available. Ask questions. Find teachers. Dig in. Understanding changes everything.

Second, conviction and joy belong together. The people wept when they heard the law, and that was right. But the leaders told them to celebrate, and that was right too. You don't have to choose between taking sin seriously and experiencing God's joy. Both are essential. Conviction without joy leads to despair. Joy without conviction leads to shallow faith. Together, they produce something real.

Third, remembering the past shapes the future. The great prayer in Nehemiah 9 retold the entire history of Israel, the good and the bad. They didn't skip the embarrassing parts. They named their ancestors' failures honestly. But they also named God's faithfulness honestly. Remembering both kept them grounded. You can't move forward well if you've forgotten where you've been.

Fourth, commitments need to be specific. The people didn't just say "we'll do better." They named exact areas where they would change: marriage, sabbath, tithes, temple support. Vague intentions produce vague results. If you want to grow, name the specific thing you're going to do differently.

Fifth, God's mercy outlasts your failure. That's the drumbeat of Nehemiah 9. "But they sinned… but you are a gracious and merciful God." The pattern never breaks. No matter how many times the people failed, God's mercy was still there. That doesn't make sin acceptable. But it does make hope possible.

TALKING POINTS

1. **The people asked Ezra to read God's word. Nobody forced them.** What do you think created that hunger in them?

What makes someone genuinely want to hear from God rather than just going through the motions?

2. **The leaders told the weeping crowd to stop mourning and start celebrating.** Is there a time when focusing too much on your failures can actually keep you from experiencing God's grace? How do you balance being honest about sin with accepting forgiveness?

3. **The Feast of Tabernacles involved leaving solid houses to live in temporary shelters.** Why would God want his people to practice being uncomfortable and vulnerable? What might it look like for you to remember your dependence on God when life is going well?

4. **The prayer in Nehemiah 9 repeats a pattern: the people rebel, but God shows mercy.** Why do you think the Bible is so honest about Israel's failures? What does the repetition of that pattern teach us about God's character?

5. **The people ended their covenant with a specific promise: "We will not neglect the house of our God."** What would it look like for you to make a specific, practical commitment to not neglect your relationship with God? What would that commitment be?

The covenant is sealed. The promises are made. The community is united, at least for now. But promises are easier to make than to keep, and the story of God's people has always been a story of good intentions that slowly unravel. What happens when Nehemiah leaves Jerusalem and comes back to find that everything he built has started to fall apart?

Turn the page.

7

THE DAY THE WALLS SANG

Mark Twain's *A Connecticut Yankee in King Arthur's Court* is the story of a man who gets the chance to rebuild a broken world. Hank Morgan, an American engineer, wakes up in sixth-century England and decides to drag the kingdom into the modern age. He builds schools, strings telegraph wires, establishes newspapers, trains people in new skills. For a while, it works. The kingdom begins to change. Hank is celebrated. His systems run. His reforms take hold.

Then he leaves. When he comes back, everything he built has collapsed. The old loyalties, the old superstitions, the old power structures have rushed back in like water through a cracked dam. The schools are empty. The reforms are undone. The people who cheered him now follow someone else. Hank is left standing in the wreckage of his own achievements, wondering if any of it ever mattered.

That's roughly what happens to Nehemiah in the final chapters of his book. After the greatest triumph of his life, after one of the most joyful days in Israel's history, he leaves Jerusalem and returns to find that nearly everything he fought for has been quietly abandoned. The promises are broken. The temple is compromised. The sabbath is ignored. The intermarriages are back.

It's the rawest ending to a book in the Old Testament. And it's exactly the ending the story needed.

FILLING THE CITY

With the wall complete and the covenant renewed, Nehemiah turned to a practical problem: Jerusalem was too empty. The city was large, the walls were strong, but there weren't enough people living inside them to defend or sustain the place. Most of the population preferred to stay in their villages, where they had farms, businesses, and established lives. The holy city was safe now, but it was also a bit of a ghost town.

The leaders were already living in Jerusalem, but they needed more families. So the people cast lots (a kind of ancient drawing names out of a hat) to select one out of every ten families to move into the city. The ones who were chosen volunteered willingly, and the rest of the community honored them for it.

That might not sound like a big deal, but it was a real sacrifice. Moving to Jerusalem meant leaving your land, your neighbors, your routine. It meant starting over in a city that was still rebuilding, surrounded by people you might not know well. The fact that those chosen accepted it cheerfully, and that others praised them for it, says something about the spirit of this community. They understood that Jerusalem wasn't just any city. It was the holy city. And keeping it alive required people willing to put the mission ahead of their comfort.

THE DAY TWO CHOIRS WALKED THE WALL

Then came the dedication of the wall, and it was glorious. Nehemiah organized two massive processions. He gathered the priests and Levites, purified them, purified the people, and purified the gates and the wall itself. Then the two groups climbed up onto the wall and marched in opposite directions. One procession, led by Ezra, went to the right along the southern wall. The other, with Nehemiah following behind the choir, went to the left along the northern wall.

Picture this: two rivers of people walking on top of the wall they had built with their own hands, the wall that the enemies said couldn't be built, the wall that a fox was supposed to knock down. Trumpets blaring. Cymbals crashing. Choirs singing at full volume. The two processions moved around the entire city, passing every gate, every section, every stone that someone had laid while holding a sword in the other hand.

Eventually the two groups met at the temple. And there, in the house of God, they offered great sacrifices and celebrated with such overwhelming joy that the text says, "the sound of rejoicing in Jerusalem could be heard far away."

Far away. The same neighbors who had mocked and threatened and plotted heard that sound. Sanballat heard it. Tobiah heard it. Geshem heard it. The noise of an entire city praising God carried across the hills and into the ears of every enemy who had said this day would never come.

This was the high point. The mountaintop. The moment everything in Ezra–Nehemiah had been building toward. The people were home. The temple was standing. The wall was complete. The Law had been read. The covenant had been renewed. The city was dedicated to God.

If the story ended here, it would be a perfect ending.

But the story doesn't end here.

NEHEMIAH GOES AWAY

After twelve years as governor of Jerusalem, Nehemiah returned to Persia as he had promised King Artaxerxes. We don't know exactly how long he was gone. The text simply says "after some time" he asked the king for permission to go back to Jerusalem.

What he found when he got there nearly broke him.

TOBIAH'S FURNITURE

Remember Tobiah? The Ammonite official who had mocked the wall, plotted against Nehemiah, sent threatening letters, and tried every trick imaginable to sabotage the building project? The man Nehemiah had looked in the eye and told, "You have no share in Jerusalem or any claim or historic right to it"?

Tobiah was living in the temple.

While Nehemiah was away, the high priest Eliashib, who was related to Tobiah by marriage, had cleared out one of the large temple storerooms, the room that was supposed to hold grain offerings, frankincense, temple equipment, and the tithes that supported the Levites, and had given it to Tobiah as a personal apartment. The enemy of God's people had moved his furniture into the house of God.

When Nehemiah found out, he didn't hold a committee meeting. He threw Tobiah's furniture out of the room.

Personally. Then he ordered the room purified and the temple equipment and offerings restored to their proper place.

THE LEVITES GO HOME

That wasn't the only thing Nehemiah discovered. The Levites, the people responsible for leading worship and maintaining the temple, had abandoned their posts and gone back to their farms. Why? Because nobody was giving them the tithes they depended on for food. The people had promised in the covenant of chapter 10, "We will not neglect the house of our God." But they had neglected it. The Levites were starving, so they left.

Nehemiah confronted the officials: "Why is the house of God neglected?" Then he tracked down the Levites, brought them back to their positions, and set up a reliable system for collecting and distributing the tithes so it wouldn't happen again.

THE SABBATH MARKET

Next, Nehemiah discovered that the sabbath had become just another business day. People from the surrounding regions were bringing loads of grain, wine, grapes, figs, and other goods into Jerusalem on the sabbath and selling them openly. Jewish families were buying. The merchants from Tyre, the ancient trading city on the coast, had set up shop right in Jerusalem and were doing brisk business on the day God had set apart for rest and worship.

Nehemiah was livid. He confronted the nobles of Judah: "What is this wicked thing you are doing, desecrating the sabbath day? Didn't your ancestors do the same things, so that our God brought all this calamity on us and on this city? Now you are stirring up more wrath against Israel by desecrating the sabbath."

Then he took action. He ordered the city gates shut before the sabbath began on Friday evening and not opened until the sabbath was over. He posted his own servants at the gates to make sure no loads of merchandise came through. When the merchants camped outside the walls overnight, hoping to wait it out, Nehemiah went out and warned them personally: "Why do you spend the night by the wall? If you do this again, I will lay hands on you." They didn't come back.

THE CHILDREN WHO COULDN'T SPEAK

The final blow was the hardest. Nehemiah discovered that some of the men of Judah had married women from Ashdod, Ammon, and Moab. The same sin that Ezra had confronted years earlier was back.

But Nehemiah noticed something that made it even worse: the children. Half of them couldn't speak the language of Judah. They spoke the language of Ashdod or one of the other surrounding peoples. These kids couldn't read the Scriptures. They couldn't understand the Law when it was read aloud. They couldn't participate in the worship that was supposed to define them as God's people. One generation of compromise was producing a generation that was losing its identity entirely.

Nehemiah's reaction was volcanic. He rebuked them. He called down curses. He pulled out some of their hair. He made them swear an oath that they would stop giving their daughters to foreign men and stop taking foreign women for their sons. He pointed to Solomon as the ultimate warning: "Was it not because of marriages like these that Solomon king of Israel sinned? Among the many nations there was no king like him. He was loved by his God… but even he was led into sin by foreign women."

Then came the final outrage. One of the grandsons of the high priest Eliashib had married the daughter of Sanballat, Nehemiah's archenemy. The priesthood itself, the holiest office in the nation, had been infiltrated by the very people who had tried to destroy Jerusalem. Nehemiah chased the man away.

"REMEMBER ME, O MY GOD"

The book of Nehemiah doesn't end with a victory parade. It doesn't end with the sound of singing on the walls. It ends with Nehemiah cleaning up messes, confronting sin, and praying a short, repeated prayer that echoes through the final chapter like a heartbeat: "Remember me, O my God, for good."

He says it after restoring the tithes. He says it after enforcing the sabbath. He says it at the very end, after purifying the priests and organizing the wood offerings and the firstfruits: "Remember me with favor, O my God."

It's not a boast. It's not a victory speech. It's the prayer of a man who has done everything he knows how to do and is leaving the results in God's hands. He built the wall. He organized the community. He confronted corruption. He enforced the covenant. But he knew, better than anyone, that walls and laws and reforms can't change the human heart. The people had made beautiful promises and broken them almost immediately. The cycle was still spinning.

And that's where the book of Nehemiah leaves us. Not with a neat resolution but with an honest question hanging in the air: if the best leaders, the strongest walls, the clearest law, and the most sincere promises aren't enough to keep God's people faithful, then what is?

WHAT THIS MEANS FOR US

First, celebrations matter. The wall dedication wasn't just a party. It was an act of worship that claimed the city for God and reminded the people of what he had done. Marking milestones, celebrating God's faithfulness, remembering what he has brought you through, these aren't luxuries. They're essential. They anchor your faith in something real.

Second, absence reveals what's real. When Nehemiah left, the community's true priorities surfaced. The promises they made while he was standing in front of them evaporated once he was gone. That's a warning: the faith that only holds up when someone is watching isn't faith. Real commitment endures when nobody is checking.

Third, small compromises lead to big collapses. Tobiah didn't storm the temple with an army. He moved in, one piece of furniture at a time, with the high priest's permission. The sabbath didn't collapse overnight. It eroded one transaction, one exception, one convenience at a time. Watch the small things. The small things become the big things.

Fourth, every generation has to choose for itself. The children who couldn't speak their parents' language are a haunting image. Faith is always one generation from extinction. It doesn't transfer automatically. It has to be taught, lived, and chosen by each new generation. Your parents' faith can give you a foundation, but it can't be a substitute for your own.

Fifth, the story isn't over. Nehemiah's prayer, "Remember me, O my God," is not the prayer of a man who thinks he has all the answers. It's the prayer of a man who knows he doesn't. It points forward to the day when God himself would provide what walls and laws and reforms never could: a heart that actually wants to obey. That day was still hundreds of years away, in a stable in Bethlehem. But it was coming.

TALKING POINTS

1. **The wall dedication was one of the loudest, most joyful celebrations in the Bible.** Why do you think it mattered for the people to physically walk on the wall and sing? What does it look like for you to celebrate what God has done in your life?

2. **When Nehemiah left Jerusalem, the community quickly broke the promises they had made.** Why do you think it's so hard for people to keep commitments when no one is holding them accountable? What helps you stay faithful when nobody is watching?

3. **Tobiah moved into the temple storeroom with the high priest's help.** How do things that don't belong in our lives sometimes get invited in by the people we trust? How can you recognize when something harmful is being treated as normal?

4. **Nehemiah noticed that the children of intermarried families couldn't speak the language of Judah.** What are the "languages" of faith that the next generation might lose if no-

body teaches them? What are you doing now that will shape who you become later?

5. The book ends with Nehemiah's prayer: "Remember me with favor, O my God." Why do you think the book ends with a prayer instead of a victory? What does that tell us about what really matters in the end?

The walls are dedicated. The promises are made and broken. Nehemiah stands in the rubble of good intentions, praying for God to remember him. And the question that Ezra–Nehemiah has been building toward from the very first verse is finally, painfully clear: if exile couldn't fix God's people, and return couldn't fix them, and the Law couldn't fix them, and the strongest leaders couldn't fix them, then who can?

The books of Ezra and Nehemiah don't answer that question. They can't. That's not a flaw. It's the point. These books stand at the end of the Old Testament story like an open hand, reaching forward across four hundred years of silence toward something they can feel coming but can't yet see.

Think about everything we've watched. God stirred the heart of Cyrus to send the exiles home. The temple was rebuilt. The walls went up in fifty-two days. Ezra read the Law and the people wept. They renewed the covenant and made specific, heartfelt promises to obey. And within a generation, every promise was broken. The tithes stopped. The sabbath was ignored. Tobiah was sleeping in the temple. The children couldn't speak their own language.

The pattern never changed. Not in the wilderness. Not in the time of the judges. Not under the kings. Not after the exile.

God's people kept failing, and God kept being faithful, and the gap between what they promised and what they could actually do never closed.

But here's what Ezra and Nehemiah show us, even without saying it directly: the problem was never the walls. It was never the temple or the law or the leadership. The problem was the human heart. And no external structure, no matter how well-built, can fix what's broken on the inside.

Many years earlier, a prophet named Jeremiah had already hinted at the answer. God told him, "I will put my law in their minds and write it on their hearts. I will be their God, and they will be my people" (Jeremiah 31:33). Not stone tablets. Not scrolls read from a platform. The law written on the heart itself, by God himself. A new covenant, one that couldn't be broken because it wouldn't depend on human willpower to keep it.

And centuries after Nehemiah's prayer echoed into silence, in the same little town of Bethlehem where Ruth had gleaned grain and where David had watched sheep, a baby was born. He didn't look like a king. He didn't come with a military escort or royal letters or a governor's authority. He came as a carpenter's son, born in a stable, wrapped in rags.

But he was the answer.

Jesus didn't come to build another wall or reform another community or enforce another set of promises that people would eventually break. He came to do what no leader in Ezra–Nehemiah could do: change the human heart from the inside out. He came to be the temple where God's presence would dwell permanently, not in a building but in a person. He came to be the sacrifice that would make atonement once and for all, ending the endless cycle of offerings that were never quite enough. He came to establish the covenant that Jeremiah dreamed of, the one written not on stone but on the hearts of everyone who trusts him.

The night before he died, Jesus lifted a cup of wine and said, "This is my blood of the new covenant." New. Not patched. Not renewed for the hundredth time. New. The kind of covenant that doesn't depend on your ability to keep it, because the one who made it also keeps it.

Nehemiah prayed, "Remember me, O my God, for good." It was the prayer of a man who had given everything he had and knew it still wasn't enough. And God did remember. Not just Nehemiah, but every person who has ever tried to be faithful and fallen short. He remembered by sending his Son to do what we could never do for ourselves.

That's where the story of Ezra and Nehemiah leads. Not to a finished wall or a signed covenant or a purified priesthood. It leads to a cross, an empty tomb, and a promise that the God who rebuilds ruined cities can also rebuild ruined hearts.

The rubble of Ezra–Nehemiah is real. The failures are honest. The unresolved ending is painful. But it's not the final chapter. The God who stirred the heart of Cyrus, who watched over the builders, who filled Jerusalem with the sound of singing—that God was just getting started.

And he's not finished with your story yet.

www.ingramcontent.com/pod-product-compliance
Lightning Source LLC
Chambersburg PA
CBHW051003050726
47592CB00007B/2688